D1511312

Whole Days Outdoors
An Autobiographical Album
by
Jim Arnosky

Photographs by

Deanna L. Arnosky

 Richard C. Owen Publishers, Inc.
Katonah, New York

Meet The Author

Richard C. Owen Publishers, Inc.
PO Box 585
Katonah, New York 10536

Library of Congress Cataloging-in-Publication Data

Arnosky, Jim.
    Whole days outdoors : an autobiographical album / by Jim Arnosky.
        p. cm.—(Meet the author)
    ISBN-13: 978-1-57274-859-0
    ISBN-10: 1-57274-859-1
    1. Arnosky, Jim—Juvenile literature. 2. Authors, American—21st
century—Biography—Juvenile literature. 3. Children's literature—Authorship—Juvenile
literature. I. Title. II. Series: Meet the author (Katonah, N.Y.)

    PS3601.R5856Z55 2006
    508.092--dc22
    [B]

                                                        2006045340

Editor, Art, and Production Director   *Janice Boland*
Editorial and Production Assistant   *Christine Ditmans*

Printed in China

9   8   7   6   5   4   3   2   1

For more information about our collection of Meet the Author books and other children's books visit our website at www.RCOwen.com or call 800-336-5588.

To Michelle and Amber

Pennsylvania

Erie

Susquehanna River

W. Branch Susquehanna River

Allegheny River

Scranton

Allentown

Pittsburgh

Harrisburg ★

Monongahela River

Gettysburg

Susquehanna River

Philadelphia

Art from *Watching Water Birds*.

I was born in New York City but raised in Pennsylvania. My youngest years were spent in a rural area outside of the city of Philadelphia known as the Main Line. It is quite different now, but when my family moved to the sleepy little hamlet of Malvern, it was very rural.

My brother Bobby and I can remember spending whole days outdoors, shoeless. We climbed trees, tracked wildlife, played baseball in unmowed fields, and swam in the muddy ponds of farm pastures.

Everything I love doing today seems to stem from those sweet pastoral times.

When I was thirteen years old, my family moved to the city of Philadelphia. It was a cultural shock. Everything was different. More traffic. More noise. More lights on the streets. More kids—and they seemed to me to be tougher than I was.

But after a little while, I made friends and did fine. It turned out that my new city friends were just as nice as my friends were in Malvern.

I went to Catholic school. We didn't have any art classes,
but I was naturally artistic. I even taught myself to play
the guitar.

My father was a patent draftsman, which meant that
he drew pictures of new machines and inventions
for the U.S. Patent Office. He taught me and my brothers
and sister how to draw. At a very young age, I could draw
anything I saw.

When I graduated from high school, I didn't want to go
to college. Instead, I got a job in a small drafting firm
as a trainee. I spent my days drawing electrical diagrams.

Soon afterward, I met Deanna. We were both 19 years old
and did everything together. She liked the outdoors as much
as I did. She even liked riding on my motorcycle with me.

During the Vietnam War I joined the United States
Naval Reserve, married Deanna, became a father,
and spent almost two years on active duty—most of it
in Germany. Deanna and our daughter Michelle came to
Germany to be with me.

When we returned to the U.S., I pursued a career as an artist
in a printing company. I also began looking for freelance work
as an illustrator.

In order to live inexpensively, we moved to a rustic
little cabin in the Pennsylvania mountains. It was there,
at the base of Hawk Mountain, that I learned all about
the forest and streams.

We were happy in our little cabin. Deanna got water
every day from a spring. I chopped our firewood.

We planted a garden and raised our own vegetables.

When our second daughter, Amber, was born,
the cabin felt a little small. We needed more room.

I was doing drawings for a number of magazines including *Ranger Rick's Nature Magazine*, *Jack and Jill*, and *Cricket*. All my assignments came through the mail, and it occurred to us that we could live anywhere.

We decided to move and went looking far and wide for a country home with wilderness nearby so I could continue my wildlife studies. We looked in Pennsylvania. We looked in New York State. We finally found our home in Vermont.

We live in an old farmhouse tucked against the mountains. The house is almost two hundred years old. And in all that time it has only had seven owners.

Here in this old house, I do the artwork for my books.

I have a small drafting table in a room in the center
of the house. We call it "the drawing room."

To add color to my drawings, I taught myself how to paint.
Most of my artwork is done in acrylic paint.
I can use the paint mixed very thin and transparent,
like watercolors. Or I can use it mixed thick and opaque,
like oils. To get the most brilliant colors, I use the paint
right from the tube with very little water on the paintbrush.
This technique is called "dry brush."

I don't like to sit at my drawing board for more
than 15 minutes at a time, so I work in short spurts.

Between spurts I get up and go outside. I may walk out to the garden or up in the woods. I may mow some of the lawn or pasture. I may take a little ride on my Harley®.

I can actually finish painting a picture and finish mowing the lawn in one day. All of my walking and hiking and mowing and riding keeps me physically fit. I have always believed that an artist should stay active, especially an artist like myself, who specializes in outdoor subjects.

I'm proud to say that I spend as much time outdoors researching my books as I spend indoors creating them.

My desire to learn about wild animals first hand, in their natural habitats, led me to photography and to videography—two tools that I use in my work to this day.

When our daughters left home to marry and have families of their own, Deanna and I began to travel, and Deanna took up photography, too.

These days we travel all over the country searching for wildlife. Deanna takes still pictures using a digital camera with a telephoto lens.

I videotape animals, plants, and scenery using a Betacam SP–the same video camera news-gatherers use. My video camera also has a telephoto lens.

Our telephoto lenses allow us to take close-up pictures of wild animals we wouldn't want to get too close to, like venomous snakes, unpredictable bison, and surprisingly quick alligators.

The photos Deanna takes and the videos that I shoot provide me with lots of visual material to work from when I create the paintings for my books.

Often when I'm afield, I'll abandon the camera and sit
and write or sketch my impressions of where I am
and what I am seeing. I carry a small pad in my shirt pocket
for these scribbles and notes.

Home again after a long research trip, Deanna and I both catalog our photos and videotapes.

I gather my field notes and sketches into my journal.
Then, I can begin to think about the book I want to make.

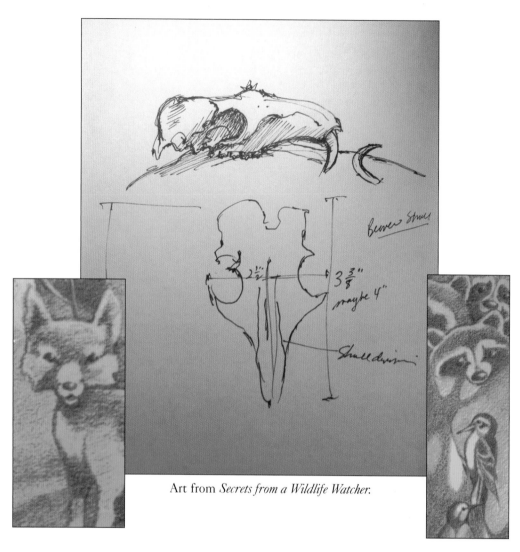

Art from *Secrets from a Wildlife Watcher*.

My artwork is based on things I really have seen.
I work in order, starting from page one, recalling all I can
for each scene. I paint picture after picture after picture.

Art from *Drawing from Nature*.

Usually when I've painted half of the pictures
I need for a book, the words start coming to me.
Then I begin to divide my days.
In the mornings, I write the manuscript for the book.
In the afternoons, I continue working on the art.

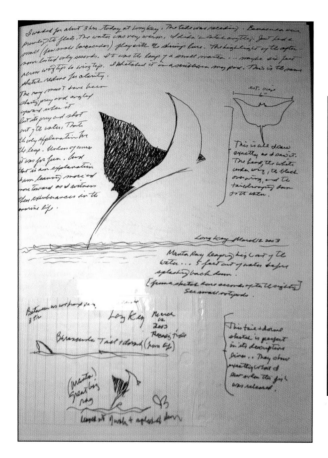

My journal writings are the freshest record of things
I've seen and done, because I write and draw in my journal
as soon as I get home from an outdoor adventure.

My writing is guided by my memory of personal
experiences and by the notes and paragraphs
and drawings that fill the pages of my journal.

Art from *Freshwater Fish and Fishing.*

The que

The queen is the mother of all the bees
that live in the hive.

Spring   (TEXT 2)

p. 8½

Hello. My name is Crinkleroot. I was
born in a tree and raised by bees. I can
find a mole hole on a bear, a fox turn in
the forest, and spot a mole hole on a mountain.
I can whistle in a hundred
languages and speak caterpillar, turtle,
and salamander, too!

Where I live deep in the forest, the trees grow
so tall they touch the sky. When I look up
at the treetops, I can feel the world slowly
turning.

Day by day, week by week, month by month,
I love to watch the seasons change. Summer.
Autumn. Winter. Spring.

When I'm working on the manuscript for a book,
my morning's output of work is limited to where I am
in painting the artwork.

I never write much more than a paragraph or two
a day. Actually, it's hard to write one good paragraph
in a morning's time.

When I finish the first draft of a paragraph, I go over it very carefully to see if I can say any part of it in fewer and better-chosen words.

Sometimes I will write outdoors, on the lawn mower, or on my boat *Crayfish*. On the lawnmower, I memorize the sentences I compose. On the boat, I write as I usually do, in free-hand on a yellow legal pad.

There are few things that I find more satisfying
than writing a good paragraph or two while bobbing
gently on the water.

I've been doing this in exactly the same way for over thirty years. I've created ninety-three books this way—both the words and the pictures.

Art from *Coyote Raid in Cactus Canyon.*

Art from *Wolves: One Whole Day.*

Art from *Every Autumn Comes the Bear.*

And all of them are about wild animals I've really seen and wild places I've really been.

Art from *Wild and Swampy.*

Art from *All About Frogs*.

Art from *Beachcombing: Exploring the Seashore*.

When I was young I loved fishing, drawing,
tracking animals, playing the guitar, and riding
motorcycles.

Art from *Crinkleroot's Guide to Knowing Butterflies and Moths.*

Today I still love to fish and draw. I play my guitar almost everyday.

And I ride my Harley Davidson® motorcycle.

I still spend whole days outdoors.

I haven't changed much.
And I hope I never do.

Jim Arnosky

Other Books by Jim Arnosky

All About Lizards; All About Owls; All About Rattlesnakes; Field Trips: Bug Hunting, Animal Tracking, Bird-watching, Grandfather Buffalo; Hook, Line, and Seeker; Shore Walking; Shore Walker; Sketching Outdoors in Autumn; Sketching Outdoors in Spring; Sketching Outdoors in Summer; Sketching Outdoors in Winter; Crinkleroot's Nature Guides.

About the Photographer

Deanna Arnosky is an expert wildlife watcher. Accompanying her husband, Jim Arnosky, on wildlife excursions, it was natural that she take up photography. Her photographs are used as reference for many of Jim's paintings. Deanna also organizes Jim's school, library, and bookstore visits.

Acknowledgments

Page 4 art from *Watching Water Birds* published by National Geographic Children's Books © 1997 appears courtesy of Jim Arnosky; Page 18 art from *Secrets of a Wildlife* published by William Morrow & Co © 1983 appears courtesy of Jim Arnosky; Page 19 art from *Drawing from Nature* published by Turtleback Books © 1987 appears courtesy of Jim Arnosky; Page 21 art from *Freshwater Fish and Fishing* published 1991 by Four Winds Press, appears courtesy of Jim Arnosky; Page 25 art from *Coyote Raid in Cactus Canyon* published 2005 by G.P. Putnam's Sons, appears courtesy of Jim Arnosky; Page 25 art from *Wolves* published 2001 by National Geographic Children's Books appears courtesy of Jim Arnosky; Page 25 art from *Every Autumn Comes the Bear* published 1996 by Putnam Juvenile, appears courtesy of Jim Arnosky; Page 26 art from *All About Frogs* published 2002 by Scholastic Reference, appears courtesy of Jim Arnosky; Page 26 art from *Beachcombing: Exploring the Seashore* published 2004 by Dutton Juvenile, appears courtesy of Jim Arnosky; Page 27 art from the cover of *Wild and Swampy* published 2000 by HarperCollins, appears courtesy of Jim Arnosky; Page 29 art from *Crinkleroot's Guide to Knowing Butterflies and Moths* published 1996 by Simon & Schuster Children's Publishing appears courtesy of Jim Arnosky; Page 31 art from *Nearer Nature* published 1996 by Lothrop, Lee & Shepard, appears courtesy of Jim Arnosky.

Meet the Author titles

Verna Aardema	*A Bookworm Who Hatched*
David A. Adler	*My Writing Day*
George Ancona	*Self Portrait*
Jim Arnosky	*Whole Days Outdoors: An Autobiographical Album*
Frank Asch	*One Man Show*
Joseph Bruchac	*Seeing the Circle*
Eve Bunting	*Once Upon a Time*
Lynne Cherry	*Making a Difference in the World*
Lois Ehlert	*Under My Nose*
Denise Fleming	*Maker of Things*
Douglas Florian	*See for Your Self*
Jean Fritz	*Surprising Myself*
Paul Goble	*Hau Kola, Hello Friend*
Ruth Heller	*Fine Lines*
Lee Bennett Hopkins	*The Writing Bug*
James Howe	*Playing with Words*
Johanna Hurwitz	*A Dream Come True*
Eric A. Kimmel	*Tuning Up*
Karla Kuskin	*Thoughts, Pictures, and Words*
Thomas Locker	*The Man Who Paints Nature*
Jonathan London	*Tell Me a Story*
George Ella Lyon	*A Wordful Child*
Margaret Mahy	*My Mysterious World*
Rafe Martin	*A Storyteller's Story*
Patricia McKissack	*Can You Imagine?*
Laura Numeroff	*If You Give an Author a Pencil*
Jerry Pallotta	*Read a Zillion Books*
Patricia Polacco	*Firetalking*
Laurence Pringle	*Nature! Wild and Wonderful*
Cynthia Rylant	*Best Wishes*
Seymour Simon	*From Paper Airplanes to Outer Space*
Mike Thaler	*Imagination*
Jean Van Leeuwen	*Growing Ideas*
Janet S. Wong	*Before It Wriggles Away*
Jane Yolen	*A Letter from Phoenix Farm*

For more information about the Meet the Author books and other children's books visit our website at www.RCOwen.com or call 1-800-336-5588